TABLE OF CONTENTS

PART 1: UNDERSTANDING THE NARCISSIST

What is Narcissistic Personality Disorder (NPD)?

In a nutshell, it can be interpreted as only the interests of the narcissist matter. In comparison, your interests don't matter because they will do whatever it takes to fulfill their needs at your expense due to restricting their capacities and external restrictions. From the victim's viewpoint, it's interpreted as violence. From the narcissist's perspective, it's perceived as simply a normal function, like stretching out a hand to pluck the fruit from the flower; you're the tree. The narcissist's motivation source is the pathology of their uncompromising desires.

What makes the tyrannical demands of the narcissist the next step is disdain. The narcissist is nonsensical unless you consider disdain. We all have desires, so we don't despise others' needs. Narcissists are contemptuous of your desires, they are contemptuous of your weakness, they are contemptuous of the fact that you still have needs, they blame you for getting them, and they strive to harm you with your needs, purposely allowing them to fail. Contempt lifts the narcissist. This ultimately causes them to undermine the trust, as trust is weakness, and vulnerability causes their disdain.

The narcissist has virtually no internal limits on abusing or abusing you unlimitedly, and they have no regard for anything; nothing is holy to the narcissist. The narcissist doesn't take anyone or something seriously because they just disrespect everything, often leading them to feel contempt or indifference about anything they inevitably encounter. They're not shameful for what they're doing, nor should you make them responsible or take responsibilities when they've never taken you seriously. They don't feel shameful or accountable to anyone; they're disdainful or indifferent. They hate your accident and your ability to know the facts. They hate your desires and feelings, disregarding both. Their invalidations often arise from their disdain for being noticed or heard.

Narcissistic assault victims also experience subtle hostility in relationships.

This, too, is the product of their hidden idea when they claim to love you. Narcissists may send off a shell of lucidity and reason, but they don't think straight because they still hate reasoning or reality. If you do your homework, you can start finding inconsistencies in their reasoning and contradictions in their statements and actions. Narcissists are master hypocrites, and in inconsistency, they still need to keep their disguise on because, without them, their callous indifference would be on the show.

Their balanced disdain accounts for certain puzzling aspects narcissists have found, like no credentials, but a need to attack experts. Also, the evident confidence and self-assurance of the narcissist aren't genuine; their disdain towards their audience is the trustworthy source.

All this disdain leaves narcissists unwilling to discern emotionally between individuals and objects; that's why you always see narcissists enjoying things and using people. Commonly, people love people and use things. You may fall into the narcissist's scheme of things as an entity in their self-absorbed dreams to achieve unspoken objectives.

What may have prompted NPD to become a trend on the internet in recent years is that NPDs leave a trail of devastation in their wake. Even this trail was witnessed separately before the internet to connect victims to compare and share the stories of life. With internet access, patients come together, and NPD awareness is growing. One of the most interesting aspects found is how similar the perspectives of most victims are. Narcissistic violence is real; statistically, it is very pleasing among victims; it is not subjective mumbo jumbo. If it were simply a theory, considering the internet, NPD might never have gained any curiosity.

Signs and Symptoms of Narcissistic Personality Disorder

Until we speak about why it's important to stand back and first look at early warning signs and indications, to know why it's crucial but to defend yourself, you need to be able to read the terrain, notice it early. Analyzing risk is never as good as ignoring it altogether.

There are early symptoms in the process, and late in the relationship, we'll note down some of the more important signs and symptoms; it's rough again, so most of the time, you'll be sure of them because they fit the predictable trend of Love Bomb-Devalue and Dump.

Early Stages of Relationship-Love Bombing Symptoms:

- They present themselves as victims, essentially telling all the negative stories that happened to them. How people mistreated and exploited them, attracting sympathy for this approach and connecting you, even more, to help them, support them, and attempt and repair them.
- Too good to be real.
- In the first interactions, you communicate emotionally with them, and they mimic all about your personality characteristics, style, preferences and sound simple as if they are the nearest person to your character from day 1.
- You're the greatest thing that happens to them; nobody knows them, everybody has exploited them, and you're their salvation.
- The giant red flag that victims can look for is Parental Negligence or childhood violence; if they share it with you, particularly too soon, running for your life, it won't end well for you.
- They're going to love to blast you, raise you on a pedestal, essentially shower you with praises, and any compliment or feeling you give them will respond back with more. They hook you up to their approval, love, adoration, and appreciation.
- They're really interested in you, telling you something about yourself, how was your day? They'll send you a lot of abnormal focus early on, start discussions first, speak to you for hours a day, win your confidence in this process, and get you addicted to the game.
- Unbearable mood swings, at one stage they're all lovely; at the other moment, they all erupt on you. You feel like you're moving on eggshells due to their erratic mood swings and they suck and rob your vitality alongside your esteem.

- They trigger trouble out of the blue as chaos brings fun to see how much you're able to handle and how much they can get away with; they create drama every day without any reason and then apologize, telling you they're overthinking. You don't know what to expect for the next second. It's their deception tactic to get you even more addicted to their game.
- They lavish you with all praise, respect, affection, compassion, concern, and they're like babies. They talk so early and want you to respond with the same stuff; that's the part they're trying to link you to their Empathy.
- Incredibly sexual at first encounter or chat, they'll try to hook you to their sexual game. If it doesn't work, they're going to be sensitive and lovely and going to insist that they remain with you.

Late Stages of Relationship-Devalue and Discard Symptoms:

- All love, adoration, respect, and care has demolished; they're cold and remote.
- Anything you do irritates them, even the jokes they used to chuckle at or the things you shared together.
- You're never enough to do anything; they keep dropping sarcasm per sentence.
- They get bored with you when they have no empathy and poor annoyance tolerance.
- You see their true face after 2-3 months that it was their performance, the person you believed they didn't live, it's an idea presented by them, their mask or façade drops off as acting takes a lot of energy.
- The love bombing continues to devalue.
- You feel like walking on eggshells, and you want attention,

love, and care. They withhold their feelings; they withhold anything, you strive to find answers, but they don't give you any straightforward answers, only bland and cold answers, never establish contact first, lies floating over your mind. Meanwhile, they tell you they're lonely, and if you inquire for clarification, you're going to get nothing, you're getting tired of wasting focus, you don't know what to expect from this partnership, all the things going on in your mind you want some clarity, where they're giving you as little to hold in.

- When you want to lift an opinion or challenge the relationship to be a two-way street, ask them why they changed, or where the older person you once knew is, call them on their acts and lies, they refuse anything, exploit you with tactics.

Watch for these Four Characteristics

- **Gaslighting:** Denying anything you're saying, they're going to strike you today, and tomorrow they're going to convince you they haven't achieved it. They realize you're not going to leave everything simple. They're going to challenge you and your patience because they know you have a strong bond with them. They will make you question yourself and your hope.
- **Stone Walling:** You pose a question as to where their emotions are, she changes the subject and never responds, you ask a question about what they believe, they tell you they don't know, you never get a straightforward answer.
- **Silent Treatments:** Every time you call them on their behavior; this is the cruelest technique they can use; they disappear and give you the cold shoulder. They disappear for days, weeks, and even months without receiving any of your calls or texts; you don't know what happened. Through this

tactic, they will avoid any liability for their acts; ignorance is their strongest weapon.

- **Projection:** Essentially, anytime you want to lift your opinion, you'll be punished for playing the victim card, convincing you that you're overthinking, even if you're confident that 100% did that. You end up explaining to them for the stuff you've never done, and they know deep down how much they're manipulating you; no matter what they're doing, they're still going to linger, and they've checked you early.

Do Narcissists Love? Love and Idealisation

Nope, they're idealizing. Let me tell you the distinction between affection and idealization.

Love: Willingness to empathize with a significant exchange of thoughts, concern, affection, love, value, and also a sincere feeling towards a person that involves emotions.

Idealization: A type of infatuation or fascination with a particular object or person; it does not contain any empathy.

The Narcissist: An adult with a body and a mind that lacks sensitivity and works on a four-year emotional basis is the average injured infant stuck in the adult body and mind that has never grown up mentally and has no idea what empathy entails from adolescence to chronic pain or violence.

The Development of Empathy: Empathy is the center of the personality; it begins to grow early in our adolescence, for example, for the child to represent the type of empathic individual that Empathy wants to gain in exchange, meaning affection, caring, consideration, respect, the importance of his or her parents. Empathy needs to be developed early in childhood; otherwise, if it does not develop, it will stagnate, and the infant will end up hollow as a shell.

WHAT MAKES A CHILD A CHILD? AND WHAT DIFFERS A GROWN-UP FROM A CHILD?

The most important thing that makes a child a child is its emotional level, whether you've found early on that the child loses emotion, for example, when it's developing, so it takes time. Likewise, a child attacks you unexpectedly and hits you in the face; you're injured. At the same moment, he laughs at his butt, and your parents tell you that it's just a kid that comes along, even if you're nuts, that's a lack of empathy; at the early stages of childhood, Empathy is underdeveloped. The grown-up has established their emotional level as they hit, for example, someone they're going to feel guilty for and lament that they later apologize for putting themselves in the other person's shoes.

What is the Narcissist Operating?

They begin with the idealization of a particular thing. Let's say an individual, once they idealize, they get a tunnel vision that becomes fascinated with that particular person because it's fresh and exciting. They still trust that they are in love with that person when they get high octane fuel from that person.

The distinction is that they don't love the person; they love the way that the person makes them feel for themselves. After some period, cracks tend to reappear as they have poor levels of boredom resistance; much like the average kid who gets overwhelmed with everything, the gap continues to emerge. Their internal fear is beginning to rise, and they are starting to doubt your worthiness, and you may not have been special, after all. And if you were the suffering that must have disappeared before now, that's going into their heads for someone new. Now they're beginning to groom new sources of supply when starting the Devaluation stage with you, which means they're trying to extract their emotions, resources, time, money, love from you.

Now, what's going to happen? When the tremendous amount of publicity has been attracted, the survivor continues to respond, not understanding what happened. They continue to ask the Narcissist questions and call them to action; they see this gesture as a huge danger to their safety. They begin to activate their defense mechanisms by exploiting a significant other to maintain their disguise or facade.

What is the Defence process? What are the Reactions?

For instance, you're calling them on their toxic behavior-they're trying to deny it entirely.

- You're asking for answers-they're not going to give you answers.
- You're hoping for a resolution—They're never going to give you closure.
- You call them on their actions-they're trying to change the subject or turn the blame on you and tell you that you're going nuts.

Bear in mind, the more the old source of supply or survivor asks, pleads, clings, the more control the narcissist feels, the more critical they feel. They have a weak ego, and the narcissist is behaving purely from the ego. Whatever the victim desires, they will withhold it because the victim has no more meaning in their minds because it has been replaced with a new enticing toy. They're not going to discard because any reaction from you would have made them the center of attention, and any reaction from you is still welcome; they feed on your reactions, be it a positive or an adverse reaction, so it makes them the center of attention. They see each person as objects; they cannot empathize with objects; any object is replaceable.

What the victims ought to remember? That it was never for them, it was just about the Narc, and they should never blame themselves for something they should accept it and step on because they were outstanding.

The Techniques Used to Manipulate the Victim as their Automatic Defensive Mechanism:

- **Gaslighting-Making**, you have questions about your sanity and vision.
- **Projection** of their feelings of inadequacy to you until their acts have been called upon.
- **Silent Treatments** – A form of passive violence used to neutralize the efforts to call them into toxic behavior, taking no blame or blame for it.
- **Stone Wall-**When you start looking for answers to change the subject or change the subject.
- **Emotional Withholds**, a type of retribution used by them if you keep them continuously calling for their toxic behavior, punishing you by denying caring, affection, attention, and treatment. Once the child loses the game, he or she refuses to play the game, or once you threaten the child with fact, he or she refuses to speak to you.

Is This Going to Happen Deliberately or Unintentionally?

This occurs as their unconscious reaction to the threat; this is their defense mechanism. A narcissist never plans to idealize another; it just happens. He never plans to devalue or dump anyone. It happens, though, because of frustration and their relentless hunger for supplies and all that's different, much as Adrenaline junkies searching for high or narcotics.

Easy Story To Enlighten Your Thoughts

For example, let's imagine a kid needs a pretty bad dog, a German Shepherd, and his mother buys him a dog, promising his mom that he's going to take care of the dog permanently and that he's going to embrace the dog forever.

The kid continues to idealize the dog because the dog is fresh and interesting; he's fascinated with the dog for a few weeks, months before he gets bored after he's bored and starts to devalue the dog because he's not fed empathy to the dog, not the emotional stage. He's leaving the dog to starve to death because he's bored, now what's going to happen? His mother takes over there to feed the dog and take responsibility for it.

Now the question is, would the child realize that he will idealize and undermine or discard the dog? Is that a plane? Not idealization and discarding happen as the baby gets bored; he would've never assumed the dog that the kid was fascinated with and would have dismissed it, nor would he ever have thought he would have glamorized the dog for a brief time.

Characteristics of Narcissist Personality

Grandiose Sense of Self-Importance

Grandiosity is the defining feature of narcissism. Rather than greed or pride, grandiosity is an excessive sense of dominance. Narcissists assume that they are exceptional or "special" and can only be recognized by such special individuals. What's worse, they're too smart for something standard or normal. They just want to interact and be affiliated with other high-level individuals, places, and stuff.

Narcissists also feel that they are better than anyone else and demand praise as such—even though they have done little to deserve it. They would also exaggerate or mislead clearly about their successes and skills. And when they talk about jobs or relationships, what you'll learn is how much they help, how amazing they are, and how grateful people are to have them in their lives. They're the undisputed star, and at best, everybody else is a bit of a player.

Lives in a Fantasy World that Supports their Delusions of Grandeur

Even though reality does not help their grandiose vision of themselves, narcissists exist in a fantasy universe powered by illusion, self-deception, and magical thinking. They're spinning self-glorifying dreams of infinite achievement, strength, brilliance, beauty, and perfect love that make them feel special and in control. These delusions shield them from feelings of inward emptiness and guilt, so they dismiss or rationalize the reality and views that contradict them. Anything that threatens to burst the dream bubble is greeted with intense defensiveness and even anger so that those surrounding the narcissist learn to proceed cautiously around their ignorance of the truth.

Needs Constant Praise and Admiration

A narcissist's feeling of entitlement is like a balloon that is steadily losing air without a constant supply of applause and validation to keep it inflated. Occasional compliments are not enough. Narcissists need daily fuel for their ego, so they associate themselves with others who can accept their obsessive craving for approval. These ties are rather one-sided. It's about what the admirer will do to the narcissist, and not the other way around. And if the admirer's devotion and praise are either disrupted or reduced, the narcissist sees it as a betrayal.

Sense of Entitlement

Since they believe themselves superior, narcissists perceive preferential consideration as their due. They really think they should get whatever they want. They still want the people around them to satisfy their single wish and whim immediately. This is their only meaning. If you're not expecting and satisfying their every desire, then you're worthless. And if you're worried about undermining their will or "selfishly" hoping for something in return, brace yourself for aggression, anger, or a cold shoulder.

Exploits Others Without Guilt or Shame

Narcissists never cultivate the capacity to connect with other people's feelings—to put themselves in other people's shoes. Or other words, they lack sympathy. In certain ways, they see people in their lives as objects—to fulfill their needs. As a result, they do not think twice about taking advantage of others to reach their goals. Perhaps this behavioral manipulation is intentional, but sometimes it is just evident. Narcissists don't care about how their actions influence people. Even if you find that out, they're probably not really going to get it. The only thing they can comprehend is their own needs.

Frequently Demeans, Intimidates, Bullies, or Belittles Others

Narcissists feel threatened if they meet someone who seems to have what they lack—especially those who are optimistic and famous. They're often challenged by people who don't crow or question them in any way. Their defense mechanism is disdain. The only way to neutralize the hazard and shore up their sluggish ego is to tear those people down. They can do so in a patronizing or insensitive manner as if to prove how little the other person matters to them. Or they can strike with slurs, name-calling, abuse, and threats to push the other person back into line.

Reasoning with a Narcissist

To understand them, you need to understand their logic. Narcissists act in the manner they do since their unique mode of logic inspires them, motivates them, and compels them. The selfish and narcissistic logic was inseparable. They can't step in anyone else's shoes; they can't see beyond their narcissistic square. They're like a programming program, inexorable, relentless, free of extraneous concerns.

Initially, this narcissistic argument is difficult to distinguish (because it is so new to us). Yet, it is pretty easy to understand when you see that it is focused entirely on thoughts and feelings. Thoughts and feelings solely drive the narcissists. This means that when they want something, they can't access logic. But there's something to that; the feelings and emotions they use to negotiate their goals just include their own emotions and feelings. Your emotions are never heard; they are meaningless, either because you don't exist as a human or because you are considered dumb. When you assert your thoughts and needs, you're going to be more complicated to block out. If they could understand the feelings, they could not be narcissists in the very first place. You're dealing with a creature who has never known about someone else's emotions before.

If a manipulative argument is presented, the narcissist cannot understand the reasoning and cannot understand the reality of the emotions and needs. Objective reasoning or the desires and emotions are unreasonably and illogical to the narcissist. Reasoning from logical reasoning or justifying your own desires seems stupid and unwise to the narcissist because something the narcissist does instantly understand is inherently stupid, and the narcissist often thinks like you are attempting to trick them by using your flawed, incomprehensible logic or prioritizing your own selfish needs. The more you try, the more unwise and foolish you look, or the more you appear to want to defraud them, the more you dig your own grave when you do that. Trying to speak sense to a narcissist makes you seem dumb or seem to be conniving to them. The only reasoning that doesn't seem stupid; the only thing they should trust is how they feel. It's a practical reality of how they feel is logical. Therefore, there can never be a bridge of awareness between you and the narcissist.

Those who can know the language of the narcissist's feelings will be able to trick the narcissist out of their residence and household. So when it comes to important problems of life, typically those that include bargaining between their emotions and the sufferings and inconveniences that they bring others, the narcissist can argue purely and exclusively about what they desire, never for what makes sense logically or if it impacts others. Narcissistic reasoning is locked inside, circular, and self-consistent by self-referencing. They make full sense to themselves but only to themselves, not even to other narcissists), and use the idiosyncratic vocabulary of their impulses and sheer subjectivity. Anything that sounds like a second language to them, and there are no shared meanings because they can't understand 'outside things.' For instance, you don't exist as an individual, and so neither will your needs (that proposition is intellectually coherent, as long as you don't actually exist).

Moreover, no one else lives anymore, but there is no objectivity, either the lack of object constancy, the philosophy of mind). That's why the narcissist can't grasp how you're mad or that this or that is unjust to anyone. The narcissists are natural solipsists. If there was no tree in the forest and the narcissist was not present, there was no sound. It didn't collapse, though, and the forest didn't exist either.

So, for example, you're in a relationship with a narcissist, and you're always saving up for a new home, the narcissist is unexpectedly buying a red luxury car, you're never going to end up having the new home. Trying to talk about the goals of a race car and a new home would irritate the narcissist. The harder you try, the less you make sense of the narcissist. The sports car looked amazing, and that's why it was bought instantly. Period. Period. The idea of a new home doesn't feel perfect. Talking about saving up for a new house doesn't make much sense and is dumb; this sort of stupid talk bothers the narcissist. You bother the narcissist with your dumb logic and selfish desires and emotions. The more you continue, the more irritated the narcissist gets because you don't make much sense; just bragging about the joy of a new car makes any sense. Criticizing sports cars leads the narcissist to devalue you, to mock you further to devalue you further. This is how the friendship began.

And that's why, when you and the narcissist enjoy mutual pleasures or views, the narcissist is such a barrel of fun. Still, when struggling with conflicts, the narcissist is impossible. The trick to understanding is that the narcissist goes for something that makes them feel good but avoids something that doesn't or makes them feel depressed. When they're fine, they're perfect; when they're bad, they're terrible.

What Causes a Person to Become a Narcissist?

Narcissistic Personality Traits are a by-product of unique childhood family environments. Both children want the consent and affection of their parents. Kids adapt to their homes, and perhaps the most effective and rational adaptation to such home conditions is to become a narcissist.

Below are several typical scenarios that may make children narcissistic.

Scenario 1—Narcissistic Parent Ideals

In this case, the infant is born in a home that is very competitive and awards just high achievement. One or two of the parents are an exhibitionist narcissist. The motto of the family is If you can't be the best, why bother?

When you're first in the competition to win the science fair or the star at the school presentation, you're full of recognition and focus. You're a failure because you don't. All in the family is meant to be special and to show that again and again. No matter how much you do, the burden is never gone.

Kids in these households don't feel permanently loved. It's hard for them to love something for their own sake because it confers status. Instead of being encouraged by their parents to discover what they want and wish to do more, they only earn systems with high achievement. Their parents are not involved in their children's "real selves," they are most interested in how their children will make the family look fine. They would like to be able to feel good to their neighbors: "Look what my child did!"

Kids who grow up in households like this feel safe and worthwhile because they are successful and accepted as the 'best.' The conditional affection of their youth and the overvaluation of high status and achievement in their home set in motion a lifelong cycle of attainment of success and confusion with satisfaction.

Scenario 2: The Narcissistic Parent Devaluation

In this case, there is a very authoritative and devaluing adult who is constantly bringing the kid down. The parent is usually irritable, readily angry, and has unrealistically high aspirations. If there are two or more twins, the parent may praise one and devalue the other. The "good one will easily become the "bad one, and suddenly a new sibling is raised. Nobody in the family feels safe, and they all spend their time attempting to quiet the explosive Manipulative mom.

The other parent is also viewed just like an infant and often belittled. When he or she argues with the narcissistic parent, the two of them are devalued. Kids who grow up in these homes are furious, ashamed, and insufficient. They are likely to respond in a few different ways to their childhood condition.

The Vanquished Child: A few of these children just give up and embrace defeat. In their teenage years, after decades of being told that they are useless, they may descend into self-hating shame-based depression. Then to relieve their inner guilt, they may attempt to lose themselves in impetuous, addictive behavior. Some of them become alcoholics and opioid addicts; others waste their days on the Phone. They never reach their ability because they were told they had none.

The Rebel Child:

These children openly ignore the message of their parents that they are "losers." Instead, they spend their lives seeking to prove to themselves the world and the devaluing parent that they are special and that their parents are incorrect. They're seeking success in whatever direction they can. Proving that they are unique becomes a lifetime task, while beneath, there is still a stern inner voice condemning any mistake—no matter how slight.

The Wretched Child:

These children grow up frustrated with the devaluing mom. Anyone who reminds them of their parents in any way becomes the object of their wrath. Even they themselves turn poisonous or malignant narcissists. It's not enough for them to do that; they have to kill as well.

Scenario 3: " The Golden Child"

These parents are typically close-up narcissists who are awkward in the spotlight. Instead, they brag about their very talented boy. Often the kid is very creative and deserves attention, but even these parents take it to insane lengths. This form of extreme idealization of an infant as flawless and unique will contribute to a superficial adaptation of the child in later life.

The Consequences of Reciprocal vs. Unconditional Love

All deserve to be treated realistically and to be loved unconditionally. If children assume that their parents respect them simply because they are unique, this may add to the underlying vulnerability. No one's going to win all the way. No one in any way is better than anyone else. Children who are idealized by a parent will continue to assume that they are lovable only because they are flawless and deserving of idealization.

Knowledge of the Mistakes and the Guilt

When parents idealize their offspring, they can be afraid to find the defects in themselves. This will lead them to try to aspire for excellence and to show that they are beautiful and capable of idealization.

Shocked Production of the True Self

In this phase, children can lose contact with their true selves and real likes and dislikes. Instead of discovering who they actually are and where their true passions and strengths lie, they can get off track and waste their time only doing stuff that they're already good at, and they hope their parents can get their approval.

The result: Much more parental idealization can lead to an imbalanced view of the self. When this happens, the kid sees all defects as intolerable and strives to be treated as flawless. It's a short hop, a skip, and a jump from here to the full-blown narcissism.

Scenario 4: Admirer of the Exhibitionist

Some kids end up in a narcissistic family where there is an airhead narcissist parent who presents them with affection and recognition as long as they respect and remain subservient to their parents. These children are taught selfish ideals but are prohibited from allowing themselves to be appreciated. Instead, their position in the family is to worship the superiority of their authoritarian parent uncritically without ever attempting to match or transcend the parent's achievement.

This is a perfect way to build Cover or Closet Narcissists. The children understand that they will gain narcissistic supplies—attention and praise—for not openly interfering with the narcissistic parent and that these supplies will be withdrawn and devalued if they openly attempt to be regarded as unique. All their importance in the family comes from serving as a boost to the

Exhibitionist parent's ego.

In adulthood, these children feel too humiliated and insecure about being secure in the spotlight, but their narcissism and self-esteem problems are less apparent to someone who may not know them well. May may well adjust to this task and lead fruitful lives in a job that includes helping a highly accomplished exhibitionist narcissist, whom they respect.

How Does a Narcissist Behave?

Narcissists are very selective of the vocabulary they use, and they try to use expressions that support their diabolical aims and raise their ego. Sometimes when their words are directed at others, they are meant to annoy and disturb their prey. They're trying to say stuff like you're too sensitive" or you've misunderstood me" to make you believe that your answer to them is unjustified and that you ought to project your own personal problems.

Or maybe they'll play their own classic "I hate drama" card as tensions escalate to suggest that you and not them are the root of nonsense when in fact, they're behind it. Narcissists are sure to have a handful of those damaging words that they enjoy, so look out for this characteristic as a strong indication that you're dealing with one.

Snipe, They're Directing/Aiming at You

You should be careful of someone who always tries to bring others down (both in their faces and behind their backs). Those dumb remarks are subtle, but they are packed with negativity. While they may not sound like anything in isolation, when they arise on a daily basis, they may be extremely harmful to the person they are being targeted at.

It's Still the Blame of Someone Else

A narcissist never feels that they've done wrong (they're gods). If someone is to blame in their eyes, they're still someone else. To accept remorse would be like an arrow in the center of a narcissist's ego, so they would attempt to transfer blame to others around them. But they blame the guy, his confounding and exhausting allegation that casts doubt in their minds and makes them feel insecure about their acts.

They're Not Afraid to Use Lies to Get their Way

They're going to take the facts, twist it, and insist that you're mistaken anytime you want and tell it like it was. They're going to make you doubt yourself. They're going to drive you crazy, your memory, and your convictions by forcing a distorted sense of truth upon you. And if you pretend to have witnesses, they will deny its existence or accuse you of making it seem foolish and devilish.

They've got Jekyll & Hyde Identities

A narcissist may be friendly and polite when he or she needs to be; indeed, this is also how they pursue friendship and more with their victims. They can only act in such a way, though when it is necessary, and the act is easily dropped when someone is hooked or enmeshed.

Why a Narcissist Acts the Way they Do?

Narcissus can be charming, charismatic, seductive, thrilling, and entertaining. They can also behave exploitatively, arrogantly, fiercely, coldly, competitively, selfishly, shamefully, cruelly, and vindictively. You could fall in love with their charming side and be devastated by their dark side. It may be baffling, but it all makes sense to consider what drives them. This knowledge saves you from their games, propaganda, and exploitation.

Narcissists have a self that is impaired or undeveloped. They think and behave differently than other people. The level of narcissism varies. Other individuals show more symptoms of more extreme lavishness, and other narcissists have less, milder symptoms. Consequently, the above discussion does not extend to all narcissists to the same degree.

Narcism Vulnerability

Despite possessing obviously powerful attitudes, narcissists are actually fragile. Psychotherapists view them as "fragile." They suffer from extreme loneliness, emptiness, powerlessness, and loss of purpose. Because of their intense weakness, they want the power to watchfully monitor their world, the people around them, and their emotions. Displays of fragile emotions such as anxiety, guilt, or sorrow, are unacceptable indicators of vulnerability in both themselves and others. Their protection mechanism protects them, but it harms others, particularly when they feel the most unsafe.

Narcissistic Disgrace

There is a poisonous embarrassment under their facade, and they could be unaware. The guilt helps narcissists feel unsafe and inadequate—vulnerable emotions that they must suppress to themselves and others. That's one factor they can't bear critique, accountability, dissension, or derogatory reviews, even though it's supposed to be positive. Instead, they are demanding unconditional, constructive treatment from others.

Awesomeness

Their secret guilt is due to their braggadocio and self-aggrandizement. They try to persuade themselves and others that they shine, that they are uniquely exceptional and the best, the brightest, the wealthiest, the most beautiful, and the most talented. This is also why narcissists gravitate towards celebrities and high-ranking individuals, colleges, corporations, and other organizations. Being among the strongest convinces them that they're better than most, but psychologically, they're not so confident.

Failure of Empathy

The capacity of narcissists to respond emotionally and communicate sufficient treatment and concern is greatly diminished. (See "Can a Narcissist Love?.") Without sympathy, narcissists can be greedy, hurtful, and cold when it doesn't serve them to be charming or cooperative. Relationships are transactional to them. Rather than listening to emotions, they are interested in fulfilling their needs—sometimes, even though it involves manipulating others, stealing, misleading, or violating the rule. While they may experience joy and desire at the early stages of a relationship, this is not loving but lust. They're known for their game-play. Their lack of sympathy often inspires them to feel the pain that they cause people, while their social-emotional intellect gives them the edge to control and abuse others to fulfill their needs.

Vacuity

Narcissists lack a positive, emotional connection to themselves, making it impossible for them to communicate emotionally with others. Their undeveloped self-resources and lack of inner resources require them to be dependent on others for affirmation. Despite their self-indulgence, they yearn for recognition and endless admiration. Since their sense of worth is influenced by what people think about them, they want to influence what others think they feel better about themselves. They use partnerships for self-enhancement and for their "narcissistic supply." But because of their inner emptiness, they are never fulfilled. Like the vampires who are dead inside, the narcissists manipulate and drain those around them.

Lack of Boundary

Mythological Narcissus fell in love with his own portrait, mirrored in a pool of water. At first, he didn't know it was himself. Narcissists metaphorically represent this. The inner emptiness, guilt, and undeveloped selves of the narcissists make them unaware of their limits. They can not experience other people as distinct entities, but as two-dimensional extensions of themselves, without emotions, because narcissists cannot empathize. Some people live solely to satisfy their needs. This is why narcissists are narcissistic and indifferent to their effect on others, particularly though they are cruel.

Narcissism Defenses

It is the defensive mechanisms used by narcissists to shield their insecurity that make relations with narcissists so challenging. The typical defenses they use are superiority and disrespect, denial, projection, hostility, and jealousy.

Types of Narcissists

Narcissism is multi-faceted and comes in a variety of forms. Narcissists can employ a number of strategies and protections to make you unsafe and ensuring that their rank and needs are met. It's easy to be puzzled, but it's important to recognize and spot what kind of narcissist you're dealing with. Recently two research groups have identified a shared function.

The Grandiose Narcissist

While there are various kinds and degrees of narcissism, for years, literature has concentrated mostly on the familiar—exhibitionist narcissists that pursue the limelight. There are the magnificent grandiose narcissists that are prominent figures and are visible in films. They are listed in the Diagnostic Statistical Manual of Psychiatric Disorders (DSM) under narcissistic personality disorder (NPD).

We should all spot such charming, thought-provoking extroverts whose arrogance and boldness are at times obnoxious and shameless. They are self-absorbed, justified, callous, exploitative, totalitarian, and violent. Any of them are sexually violent. These unsympathetic, narcissistic narcissists think so well about themselves but spare no contempt for anyone.

Helped by their extraversion, they report high self-esteem and happiness with their lives despite the suffering of others. Since they outwardly desire acclaim, publicity, and dominance, grandiose narcissism is outsourced. Even in love, they're hunting for strength by playing sports. Many sustain partnerships, considering the lack of affection and unhappiness of their spouses, who are quickly seduced by their charm and boldness.

The Vulnerable Narcissist

Little identified are insecure narcissists (also referred to as underground narcissists, closets, or introverted narcissists). Like their grandiose kinsmen, they are self-absorbed, justified, exploitative, unsympathetic, manipulative, and violent, but they are so fearful of scrutiny that they shy away from scrutiny. Individuals in both forms of narcissism also lack autonomy, have imposter syndrome, a poor sense of self, are self-alienated, and unable to regulate their setting. However, vulnerable narcissists perceive these things to a far larger degree.

Unlike grandiose narcissists, rather than feeling secure and self-satisfied, insecure narcissists are unsure and dissatisfied with their lives. They're feeling more pain, fear, remorse, sadness, hypersensitivity, and embarrassment. They are in disagreement, maintaining both inflated and pessimistic irrational expectations of themselves—the latter that they place on other people, their lives, as well as the future. Their negative feelings represent a bitter neurotic aversion to personal development. They need affirmation of their grandiose self-image and are extremely defensive when perceived feedback causes a poor perception of themselves.

They ignore meaningful relationships, unlike extroverted narcissists. Instead of boldly dominating others, they are threat-oriented and distrustful. Their form of attachment is more avoidable and nervous. They detach from others with violent shame and anger, internalizing their narcissism. Empathetic co-dependents feel compassionate and try to spare them from their suffering, but end up self-sacrificing and feeling responsible for them.

The Communal Narcissist

Far more challenging to classify is the third form of narcissist named only recently—communal narcissists. They admire comfort, compassion, and elegance. They see themselves and want others to see it as the most reliable and friendly atmosphere, and they seek to accomplish this through kindness and kindness. They're going out like a grandiose narcissist. But while the grandiloquent narcissist wants to be seen as the smartest and most powerful, the communal narcissist wants to be seen as the most gifted and helpful. The vain selflessness of communal narcissists is no less selfish than that of a grandiose narcissist. They both share common motivations for grandiosity, esteem, entitlement, and strength, though each employs different activities to accomplish them. It's a bigger plunge as their hypocrisy is revealed.

The Malign Narcissist

Malignant narcissists are known to be at the end of the spectrum of narcissism because of their brutality and aggressiveness. They're cynical, immoral, and sadistic. They take joy in causing confusion and dragging people down. These narcissists are not inherently grandiose, extroverted, or neurotic, but they are closely linked to psychiatry, the dark triad, and anti-social personality disorder.

Fluctuating States of Ego

If you have a hard time recognizing which sort of narcissist you're working with, that could be because grandiose narcissists are oscillating between states of grandiosity and weakness. For example, grandiose narcissists can exhibit insecurity and emotionality (usually anger) when their performance is reversed or their self-conception is under threat. More fantastic grandiosity suggests greater uncertainty and the possibility of variability. There is no proof that vulnerable narcissists display excellence.

The Search for the Core of Narcissism

Recent studies have begun to distinguish a singular, unifying characteristic between narcissists. Researchers looked at narcissism by examining distinct personality characteristics. Two recent models have emerged: one based on individuality and the other on an open, transactional leadership style.

The Trifurcated Model

The Trifurcated Model of Narcissism reveals that narcissism relies on three personality traits: agentic extraversion, discomfort, and neuroticism. (Agentic extraverts are authoritative and bold go-getters who occupy positions of acclaim, success, and leadership.) Of the Big Five personality characteristics, disabling is the only one common to all styles. The paradigm sheds light on the nature of narcissism as emotional antagonism, shared by grandiose and fragile narcissists both. It is characterized by coercion, aggression, entitlement, callousness, and rage (Kaufman et al., 2020). Vulnerable and majestic narcissists express antagonism differently. The former is more aggressive while distrustful; the latter are more immodest and powerful.

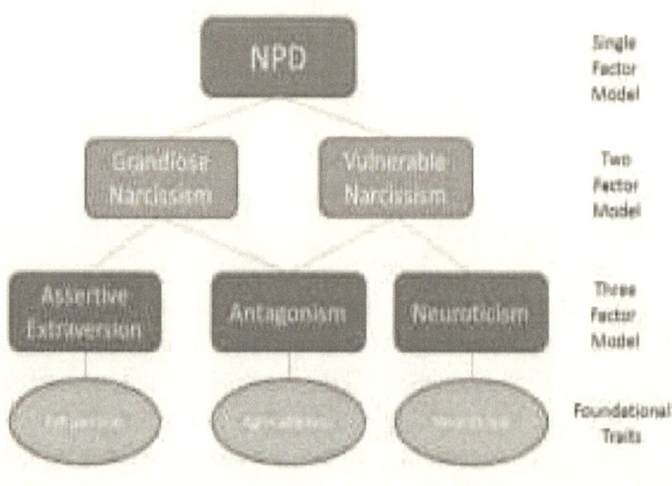

The Spectrum Model

The Narcissism Continuum Model (NSM) developed by Kerzan and Herlache (2017) conceives of narcissism as occurring on a spectrum from grandiose to fragile. It illustrates how the NPD differs in magnitude and how the traits present themselves. The model indicates that all forms of narcissists have a similar psychological center of self-importance. Narcissists believe that they and their interests are unique and that they take priority over those of others. This essence consists of greed, self-involvement, and entitlement. In reality, entitlement is reported to be the most toxic factor in relationships.

Narcissism Spectrum Model

<u>Entitled Self-Importance</u>

Grandiose Narcissists   Vulnerable Narcissists

The multiple identities of narcissists convey varying qualities at different moments; this model captures a complex, systematic study that is more reflective of real life. The greater the grandeur of an individual, the less fragile they are and vice versa. More privilege and risk-taking raise professional and emotional challenges. The greater the weakness, the more away (, the lower) is their grandiosity.

Takeaways

In brief, narcissism occurs on a continuum ranging from dominant and extroverted to introverted and neurotic. The central characteristics of narcissism are antagonism, self-importance, and entitlement, rendering narcissists unfavorable, uncooperative spouses, and work colleagues. Since other forms of personality may be antagonistic, I favor the Continuum Paradigm, which defines self-important superiority as the center of narcissism, separating it from sociopathy and paranoid personality disorder, among others.

Grandiose narcissists are presenting a mixed bag. Although they feel and work differently than vulnerable narcissists and can be socially active when they want, their antagonism and entitlement causes issues and endangers relationships. When they are taking part in counseling, they should focus on their antagonism and privilege.

On the other hand, vulnerable narcissists require assistance in controlling their attitudes, moods, and feelings. They mimic individuals with borderline personality disorder and may benefit from dialectical behavioral treatment that is effective in mitigating antagonism. Schema-focused psychotherapy and cognitive behavioral therapy are effective for all styles of minimizing guilt and anger.

Whatever sort of narcissist you care for, your friendship is hurtful. Instead of fulfilling your desires, you are weakened and drained by frequent criticism, callousness, aggression, requests, and legitimate aspirations. Don't waste your time trying to impress or change a narcissist. Instead, launch the healing to restore your self-esteem and autonomy and make you more resilient whether you stay or go. While you are undecided, take some person psychotherapy and use the Narcissist Dealing Methods to assess the relationship's prognosis.

PART 2: HANDLING THE NARCISSIST

Identifying a Narcissist

People with Narcissistic Personality Disorder are incredibly difficult to spot. And trained psychologists who have no first-hand experience (as a victim) are easily tricked. One of the world's foremost rehabilitation professionals, he was himself a working psychologist before he fell victim to a sexual narcissistic relationship – and his world turned upside down. But how on earth can anyone decide whether or not they have a narcopath on their hands?

Machiavelli

All successful con artists need brilliant tricks to get away from their audacious deceptions, and the narcopath is no different. They will be proud of their unscrupulous and treacherous ways of demanding stage appearances by an accomplished performer, but the narcissist has been honing his acting abilities since early childhood. Although others are never in the ranks, the unfortunate fact is that many are professionals and carry out their positions with distinction – literally. They are to all intents and purposes, the very cornerstone of society-in commissions, an active member of the Church, with occupations as distinguished as they can be.

Look Tough Then look at it again

Although there are a variety of indications where, if you are cynical enough to press hard, you should be given a fair hint, cunning and deceptive as they can be, these are the red flags I'm looking for.

Loving Bombarding

Narcissists know that they have to get you hooked and addicted before they continue to extract their manipulative supplies from you. They're doing this with love-bombing. Expect lots of compliments, daily texts, and messages of undying affection and desire. Right from the get-go, they intend to manipulate the mind on an hourly basis. This plays a secondary role – the growth of your confidence in someone else. Messages of sound very familiar and not actually personalized directly to you – and that's because they're not real or original, but they're copied from movies, books, and the like. Don't forget; Narc's simply don't have the same feelings as normal-range people do because they can't experience affection. So you're being courted by the same charade that's their whole life.

The Mirror

By mirroring, narcissists put themselves as the soul mate. Anticipate a lot of in-depth questions in the early days when they get to know you. Getting to know one-other is common in a relationship, but with a narcissist, it's more like research, and it's really one-sided. They're not going to give it away until you've shown it first. Then they will claim to enjoy all the same stuff as you do – activities, past-times, games, passions, music, food, places to visit, drinks, etc.

A lot of Elegance

They know how to win people over easily, and they're going to come off really charming – but for those people who count.' Expect the vicary to be handled very differently from the garbage collector. The charisma, though, is fake – something that their "false self" uses to give the appearance of a decent person, a cornerstone of civilization. Their romantic partners are only really seeing their charming sides in public – in secret, giving up hope now.

Great Ego

This is the characteristic of an accessible narcissist – brash, full of his own successes, disrespectful of others, dismissive of mistakes, unaccountable for his cock-ups, vane, and excessively preoccupied with his picture. Many would be able to see politicians and actors slipping into these stereotypes. But beware, while this may be a crucial gift to open-minded narcissists, many other types of narcissists do not suit this template. Also, with the hidden ones, though, once you get to know them personally, you're going to have this intense sense that in their lives, it's all about them.

Nice Listener

Don't mistake this one for the warm and kind type of listening and empathizing – the narcissist's way of listening is more thoughtful to research. In the beginning, narcos are searching for ways to get their hooks into you, indications of vulnerability, a hint of the narcissistic fuel tank that you serve, what makes you tick, etc.

Fast to Intimacy

The standard spectrum of individuals give time for their feelings to grow – and these emotions come naturally. Less so for the narcissist, who actually cannot sense the intimacy of feelings. They're on a supply-derived mission, and they're very irritated with normal-range objectives taking their time.

Sexually Excessively

Although they might not be willing to experience affection, sexual conquest is a validation and thus a selfish source of drugs. So expect them to be sexual until your degree of intimacy is properly built.

A lot of Crazies

Narcs are leaving a trail of devastation in their tracks. Yet they themselves cannot be kept responsible for this state of affairs – so it must be their victims, right? Look out for the narco to dismiss their exes and so on as nuts or to make a screw loose. And they're always abusive – they're masters of transferring their own flaws into their victims.

High Mood

Although they may be trying to impress you and behave themselves accordingly, they never seem to have a rather haughty attitude – particularly to people like restaurant waiters. Look for self-importance, pomposity, rudeness, and self-improvement.

Controlling the Situation

They have to monitor circumstances, particularly their spouse and children, household finances, social responsibilities, family plans. Just those that they can confidently monitor are allowed to join their core group of friends. Those who demonstrate critical thinking and independent thinking are kept at a distance.

Lack of Genuine Apology

Narcopaths are struggling to repent, really about something. They simply can't be mistaken – admitting that it dents their sense of a perfect "false self." They either freeze, change the subject, or else dodge, or mumble an apology followed by a "but... ".

You're working on Eggshells

In normal friendships and partnerships, the connection should be solid enough to feel secure that you could disagree or tell them any truths about your home. For a narcopath, you can sense an unwritten law and intestine sensation where you don't question them. Ever ever. What's more, they can also smell the mood that they're furious and on the brink of the blast, so you have to step cautiously.

Core of Focus

Narcopaths enjoy being the focus of attention and hate being cared about by someone else-especially members of the same sex. Their favorite subject of discussion is, you guessed it yourself. They're going to aspire to sit in the middle of a huge dining table, and they're going to be the first to dance on the chairs, they're going to expect high spirits at events.

Sycophant

Narcs enjoy being considered to be synonymous with higher-intellectual individuals – but perversely hate being eclipsed by them. They are especially suspicious of someone who could be found more beautiful than they are.

Lack of Continuity of Object

Like a chameleon, narcos can be customized to better shine based on the organization or the condition they are in. Invariably, behind closed doors, they would treat their closest and dearest accordingly. So whether it's their political affiliation, hobbies, preferences, favorite food, or hue – expect things to change any time the wind blows.

Achievement by Robbers

Their mixture of laziness and entitlement, and given the charade of fake selves, you will find that they are great at declaring the hard work and success of others as theirs. Those are the managers who are hard taskmasters to their subordinates while they are too busy brown-nosing their elders and winding and dining customers to roll their sleeves. Those are the partners who miss domestic tasks when they're too busy somewhere else, somewhere else. There are the couples who bum all day and trust the other half of them to get the bacon around.

Above the Rule of Law

Their lack of sympathy for people spreads to a broader culture – no one else. Connect to that their propensity for risk, their pathological lies, and their sense of superiority, and you can understand why an estimated 25 percent of the prison population has NPD.

100 Ways to Know if You are a Victim of Narcissist Abuse

1. You've got the gut sense that something is wrong, that there is stuff you don't know about.

2. You hear contradictory stories about them that don't make any sense.

3. You're going to trap them in lies, like lies that wouldn't make much sense to say.

4. You think them nice to the people you hear them talk ill of when they're not around.

5. Not only are they angry over small things, including things that don't sound rational or make sense. You can't imagine that anybody's going to get mad over that stuff, even though they're just having a bad day. The rage is coming out of nowhere.

6. You find yourself doing something you've never done in the past or experiencing things in reaction to a partner's actions that you've never felt in comparable circumstances with others or in the past.

7. You're always being accused of stealing.

8. When you try to involve them in a discussion about something that happened in a relationship that you find unjust or hurtful, the conversation turns into nonsense, and they end up turning it around on you and accusing you of initiating an argument.

9. One upon a time, the love-bombing was over the top, and you thought you had found a soulmate.

10. Their acts do not reflect the terms they utter much of the time.

11. They're going from loving you to hating you immediately, or they're suddenly going to say you don't exist.

12. They barely show regret; even if they do, they go back to doing the same stuff they said they were guilty of.

13. You're separated from the ones you care about most.

14. They talk poorly about people or things you care about, and they threaten you to stop people or things like that.

15. They stay in close touch with you while the two of you are not together, and they clothe it as being concerned."

16. They're looking for hidden nuances in what you've said, and they're taking neutral stuff as critique.

17. They always change plans for you then want you to change yours when the hat drops.

18. You see them manipulating knowledge, only letting out enough and/or saying something to people to get what they want.

19. You find yourself wary of strangers you've never met because of what you've been taught about.

20. They do terrible stuff, but somehow they have an excuse for it.

21. You're getting nervous when you're with them, uncertain of how they're going to respond.

22. They talk to people they always say they can't get up and look like you're mad when you bring it up.

23. You find yourself protecting them or shielding their horrible acts from others.

24. You don't want to call their actions manipulative, or maybe it doesn't feel like being exploited – it just sounds so overwhelming.

25. When they go, you're desperate to miss them and don't understand why.

26. You sound like you have a special bond with them.

27. They're going to make you be in regular touch with them while you're out with your friends.

28. They've got a phone full of people they've been in relationships with in the past or people they've just met, but don't want you to have friends at all, especially the opposite sex.

29. You can't concentrate on something except being obsessed with trying to figure out the friendship.

30. You find yourself trying to pick between pushing them on petty lies or letting it go.

31. Some of the lies they're telling are so vast, and they encompass having completely separate lives and making people for themselves who don't exist.

32. You feel like you're losing your mind.

33. They bait you to respond and then use your response to make you feel as though you are to blame for the death of the relationship or as if you deserve to be handled.

34. They're using stuff that you told them against you, and they're saying other people things that you told them confidently.

35. You're going to be mentally ill with no clarification.

36. You lost your self-esteem.

37. You have lost your employment, financial status, or other simple means of survival, or ways of sustaining yourself.

38. They pushed you to do stuff you didn't want to do.

39. They've made threats to hurt you physically or mentally.

40. People have turned against you in your life because of your friendship.

41. They enabled you to indulge in deviant conduct and then threatened to use it against you.

42. You're going to go, but you can't stop talking to them.

43. You want them to leave you alone; however, you want them to get in touch with you.

44. They're intruding on your privacy.

45. They waste a long time in the shower, making excuses for what they're doing there.

46. You start disassociating or withdrawing.

47. You still know like something is wrong.

48. You're sexually assaulted, so you're considered too emotional.

49. You're always on the verge, and there's no rhyme or explanation that a good night will instantly change everything that has been said. It'll set them off instinctively, and a nice night with them would suddenly turn into a nightmare. Then they pretend that it never happened, not apologizing for their actions.

51. Anything, but you don't have to do the same thing.

52. You catch yourself apologizing, even if you're not exactly what you've done anything.

53. You also feel as if they clash with you or are jealous of you and try to undermine you.

54. You always feel like they see you smiling because they're not the source; they want to do something to spoil it. Holidays, birthdays, and special days always end with pain.

55. You're full of questions, and you never get any answers.

56. Sometimes, you're not able to pick what you want to watch while they're present because when you are, they're mocked or punished.

57. They push you to hang out with their mates. However, they can place you in a double bond by accusing you of being unfriendly if you don't communicate enough with your friends or flirting if you interact "too much with them.

58. They also have cheating or psychotic exes who have treated them poorly in the past to justify why they are behaving so badly towards you today, along with several other reasons. More possibly, they produced the "crazy ex, who was actually manipulated and not psychotic.

59. They often compare you to past exes, preferably at first. Deeper in the relationship, in order to make you feel unsafe, they can continue to associate you unfavorably with exes in order to influence your actions and get you to do something or not do something. "My ex has never done that or "My ex has always done that..."

60. You often feel like your partner is two different people, and you're constantly trying to figure out which one is the "real" one.

61. Their reaction to being questioned is smug indignation, not regret.

62. They respond with frustration when they feel that you've kept something secret from them or haven't involved them in a decision or operation.

63. They deliberately keep secret some of their actions and emotions.

64. You are not permitted to have regular human responses or feelings to typical events.

65. Usually, their reaction to your feelings is to quit or place the attention back on themselves.

66. When they feel like you've wronged them – whether you have it or not – they're going to find a way to blame you for it.

67. They're behaving one way in public and another way in private because you're the only one there.

68. You find justifications for their actions, such as, "He's just a passionate person," or He's been hurt so much in the past," or He's just having a bad day."

69. Your friends and family told you that you should get away from him or her or that you're not the same person you used to be.

70. You're always looking forward to the "good old days" that prevailed when you first met your girlfriend.

71. Often, you're terrified of your mate.

72. Often, you feel really bad, and sometimes you don't even know why.

73. Your companion is a chronic liar.

74. Your companion is excellent at making his or herself a suspect, and you've discovered that he or she would also cheat you to do so.

75. Your wife has threatened to kill you or yourself if you leave your relationship.

76. Your wife has threatened to have the police involved if you left the relationship or have made any direct threats to your life or well-being if you said you would leave.

77. Your wife is trying to dictate how you look, where you go, or how you spend your time.

78. They're quitting the relationship every time they don't get the answer they expect, but they're still coming back because every time you feel like you have to give up more and more of yourself if you want them to stop doing that. You know this means that, for example, you have to avoid telling them about those topics.

79. When you show feelings or weep, often they have almost no emotion at all or even appear irritated or sometimes entertained by your discomfort.

80. They vanish for days or weeks at a time and become unreachable, and you don't know where they are.

81. Your life is full of confusion and drama, and you don't understand why it never seems to be over.

82. You sound like you're losing yourself in a friendship.

83. You no longer know yourself.

84. Your life feels like it's at a standstill. You no longer have any hobbies or other passions. Your whole life revolves around them.

85. You sound like you're going nuts.

86. You may have considered suicide because you can't work out how to leave the relationship.

87. You mean, something is really wrong, and you knew something was wrong with them a long time ago, but you can't seem to get your mind around what or why they can't just stop behaving like that.

88. The relationship has changed, and you're not sure why or how, but details that were all right at the beginning of the relationship are not. It's like it's all twisted inside out.

89. Often, they're behaving like the person you know and pledge to improve, and you're curious if it would be different this time, but there's still a feeling of doubt that they're always up to the same things they've always been.

90. You don't take care of something and don't take care of anything—your life, your relationship, your partner, the world—and you just want to take care of stuff.

91. You're also advised that things you say and do are false.

92. You're arguing about the same thing over and over, and they just seem to be able to put themselves in your shoes and appreciate your viewpoint.

93. They do things you're not "allowed" to do.

94. They make you feel guilty about things that have never happened before or for having regular human responses to insane circumstances.

95. You find yourself playing an investigator, and you have such a deep gut instinct that the stuff they're telling you are lies, and you're beginning to figure out what they're doing.

96. You have thoughts that don't match the emotions you have; for example, you feel like you want to leave the relationship, but for some reason, you think you should stay close to them.

97. They treat you as if you're inferior to them, and you don't owe things like explanations or dignity.

98. They're rewording what you said and turning your words into meanings that you never meant, and no matter what you say, you can't persuade them that it's not what you meant or intended.

99. They make what you want to do too uncomfortable or impossible if you want to do it by doing a lot of things on this list, much of which could have gone unnoticed for a long time). Later, they insist they never stopped you from doing it, leaving you to feel uncertain over why you felt like they were stopping you.

100. You sound like you're going to lose your sanity.

Handling a Narcissist Boss

It can be very difficult to work with a manager who seems to be recovering from the NPD. Though you do not know for sure whether anyone else fits the requirements for a psychiatric diagnosis, you are likely to be well aware that they show the following types of characteristics:

- Insistency on being "right" all the way
- Can easily move from one extreme to treating you as the greatest worker on the planet, and the next moment may be trying to fire you in front of the board of directors, and back again on the basis of their present attitude and how they feel about you right now.
- Failure to cope with any conflict or assertion that there may be another way to do things, even though they brag about their "open door" policy.
- Lack of object constancy (for example, when they're upset with you, they may behave as though they can't recall any past good emotions about you and/or your job, and they may even try to fire you when they're angry with you).
- In need of continuous admiration, paired with excessive prevention and/or punishing actions when they do not feel adequately admired, otherwise shamed, embarrassed, or disrespected.
- They are frequently comparing employees who might also appear to be accidentally or deliberately pitting them against

each other, often causing discord, animosity, and loss of solidarity within employees who are often focused solely on preserving their own careers.

- Can be highly aggressive, with people who work with them with people on their side, or even with their own supervisor.

Many people spend so many hours at work that their relationships with their supervisor, the way they feel about their performance, and their external opinions about it can be very critical to the overall emotional health and self-esteem.

Although all of this may be accurate, it's not really practical for people to leave their jobs, nor do they really want to, and asking the boss about it may lead to reprimand or firing. If your objective is to stay at your current job and do your best to coexist with your new employer, here's the bare bone version of mine.

Tips for Dealing With A Narcissist Boss:

Aim to make them look pretty good:

This could include moving above what they want (even though they ask in an irritating way), not giving them a bad mouth to superiors (even though they egg you on and being invaluable to them.

Research and Excel in what is Important to Them:

Your manager is likely to have special tasks that they like handled correctly ("or else") and other things that are very negative to them. Study what these items are and behave accordingly (even though it sounds stupid or unimportant to you).

Using Emotional Toolbox:

It can be very hard to be frequently insulted, no matter how hard you try, treated like trash, whether the manager is in a poor mood, or flipped to the drop of a hat. For this cause, it is really important to be extra kind to yourself and to do things that can make you feel stronger and preserve your self-esteem in this tough environment. This could include: constructive self-talk, taking brief breaks to breathe, and re-grouping, leaving early or remaining late when your supervisor leaves so that you can work better while it's quieter, preparing enjoyable activities for yourself before or after work, making time for exercising (even if it's a fast stroll around the block at lunch), etc.

Work to Stop Harming them Narcissistically

Bosses who suffer from NPD are particularly susceptible to narcissistic damage and are typically unable to cope calmly with something that feels: confrontational, humiliating, insubordinate, rude, or otherwise insulting. Of course, no one loves these emotions, but narcissists seem to respond especially violently and adversely, and it is doubtful that the object would be consistent in matching these kinds of negative feelings with some previously favorable ones about you, sometimes making them feeling negative about you and your work.

Keep Concentrated on the Objectives:

A lot of people may conclude that it's not worth getting their manager to deal with this everyday activity. On the other hand, this work may be an important move ahead in your future, or it may have other beneficial advantages that help you decide to continue. This is an independent decision for a person to make, regardless of what other people think is the right thing to do If you chose to stay, it would be immensely useful to make a list of all the stuff you're going to get out of leaving, how this work suits your needs in every way and the advantages you have of dealing with it. On days when it is especially difficult to work with your manager, please refer back to your list of reasons why you want to work there. This will act as a reminder that you're not only the villain here but that you can instead continue to concentrate your attention on the rewards of being there with you.

It can be incredibly difficult to function with a narcissist and to cope with the possible negative emotional consequences for you—the self-esteem, your level of fear, etc. The good news is that the more you learn about NPD and its general emotional and behavioral trends (as well as the particular patterns, interests, idiosyncrasies of this person), the more predictable your supervisor can get, and it's typically easier to deal with them. Assuming you plan to remain in your current position, note that this is your decision, you can set your limits, and most importantly, just because your boss calls you crazy, it doesn't necessarily mean you are.

Life with a Narcissist Partner

The narcissism will leave you feeling like you have met your true friend and soul mate. Everything's going to go fast. He's going to seem to fall in love quickly, and he's going to step in fast. At first, he might ask you to keep your relationship a secret because someone else in his life is over-controlling, doesn't approve of you, etc. And he doesn't want them to try to ruin this wonderful friendship that the two of you have with their envy or animosity.

Yet he's on the agenda. During this time, you should be confident that there is another woman in his life who is trapped with him in the evaluation process, and she has no idea about you. And she's not going to find out until she can work out how to make your relationship public, in the most dramatic, most hurtful way imaginable, during her discard. He's not going to be happy to break up with her, he's going to kill her, and you're going to be the tool he's going to use to do that. And deep down, that's just what he believes women deserve.

During the love-bombing, he'll tell you that you're different from any other woman in his world. He's going to complain about the other women, how needy they are, how mad they are, how usually feminine they are but not you. You're a special man. Well, you understand him. You're more than a human. He never thought, and will never see, any woman the way he feels for you.

And then, mysteriously, things appear to change. And with every step of the transition, your soul will be torn down a little further until you feel like a hollow, worthless shell as it sets you up for devaluation and discarding.

It's starting slowly. You start to be omitted first. And if you get angry, he tells you that it's not his fault; it's because the other people he's dealing with or friends with are jealous of you and don't understand. They're just trying to spare their emotions. If it were up to the narco, you'd be included, of course.

He's trying to motivate you to act the way he needs you to behave. He's going to thank you for the actions that would eventually make his plans simpler. He would admire your willingness to trust him enough to allow him independence, to sit at home, and to take care of the girls, so that he can go out and deal with his jobs. And it's still "work" regardless of whether it really is, how late it's going, how long it's going on, or how many days or continents it's going on. He's not on a break with his friends, and he's on a business trip. No matter what images your friends share on social media, you can be led to believe.

If you had any arguments with the narco, either he will flat out refute what he said or what he did, or he will accuse you of misinterpreting him since you're a typical woman and unable to understand what he really said. What you hear is what you think he meant. You're never listening to him. He's not unwise with you; you're unwise with him.

It's just about the projection, the gaslighting, the deflection of the narco. If he does to you, he's going to accuse you of doing to him. And he's going to tell everyone around you if he feels they're important enough.

If somebody is already talking about you until he's done (which they obviously won't be), you might learn that you're the one lying to him, that you're gasping him, that you're blaming him without evidence, that you're short-tempered with him that you're whining to friends about him that you're trying to turn people against him that you're trying to manipulate him, that you're trying to ruin his life and his livelihood, that's everything he's ever received. The list keeps moving on and on. This is a projection, and you should be confident that all the accuses you of doing to him is what he does to you, whether you know it or not.

And if you do or utter something that displeases the narco during your relationship together, it will make you regret it. He's going to get his pound of meat when he catches you and harangues you for hours on the smallest offense—for your own benefit, of course, to get you back in line. If you try to turn that into a two-way conversation, it'll piss him off even more, and the dressing-down can take another day or longer.

What he wants is for you to say he was right, you were wrong, and to feed him your guilt. And then note that he's always right, you're always wrong, and you're always mindful of your position. If you succeed in entering into some sort of discussion with the narco, you won't listen to the complexities of your argument or really know what you're really doing. He's going to skip straight to the worst situation, the most drastic circumstance possible, as a way to show, once and for all, that he's right and you're wrong.

Or he's going to respond to you with such a convoluted exercise in word salad that's too off the top and ridiculous and impossible to understand (or read), it's just better to agree with anything he says and not criticize him again ever, rather than having to go through all that again. And you can find that he begins to use amorphous 'others in his critique of you. Some people have observed your behavior. Some people have been complaining about you. Some people dislike you, and they're all your FAULT.

You're the source of all evil. You're bad. You're a bad guy, man. You're a hollow skeleton, and ALL OF That IS YOUR FAULT. And it's not just him that notices this in you. They're what he knows. Really, if it wasn't about him, you wouldn't have any friends at all. He's the one that goes on smoothing the route. He's the one who really needs to apologize to you and make excuses for you. He's the one that stops these amorphous others from even understanding how bad you are and disdaining you any more.

Around this time, he will also continue to be more discreet and then accuse you of not being available to him. He's not going to tell you what he's doing or where he's going, but he's going to ask you to tell him anything and then accuse you of never telling him. He's trying to suggest that if you don't tell him, he doesn't have to inform you about it. And if you wrote it all down on the family calendar, like he asked, well, how was he supposed to know? He's a young, important guy; he doesn't have time to review his calendars.

Then he starts securing the secret and makes sure that his computer, iPad, and phone are never left where you can reach it. Ok, congratulations. You're in the midst of the devaluation of hell.

And one day, when you walk into his party of friends, you're going to feel the glares and knives in your back. Some can also turn around and walk away from you. And you're starting to wonder what the heck you've ever done to them. Especially if you felt they were friends of yours too. They're not there.

The narco has been running to his groupies on a regular basis, telling them how abusive you are, how psychotic you are, how awful you are, how dishonest you are, how micro-managing you are, how you take advantage of him all the time, how you never listen to him how you need to be handled and monitored, or how you could ruin his life and his future.

He's going to take everything and anything you've ever said out of proportion and then exaggerate everything to the extent of becoming unrecognizable; the better he's going to flog you with it. After being rejoiced about how awful you are, how horrible you've always been, and given these distorted, exaggerated descriptions of what you're meant to be doing, they're going to endorse him one hundred percent. And then he'll use that encouragement to tell you he's clearly right about you because of look at how many people he's got on his side.

By the time it's over, the narco would have totally ruined your reputation and whatever emotions of friendship those mates might have felt for you.

And they're his mates now and just his own. To the women, the narco is coming across as this vulnerable little boy who wants to be mothered and cherished and shielded from the huge, evil of you. To the guys, he's a comrade in arms who are being victimized by a slut, and they're going to have to band together.

And he'll have done all this for a surprisingly long time—after all these seeds have to be deliberately planted—and all behind your back. That way, he's able to get his next source of supplies on the hook-like your former friend who only wants this sad little lost boy to be his mum. When he's got her well and truly addicted, and he's in a relationship with her, he will plunge further into the devaluation and dump you, and do so in the cruelest way he sees fit.

And you stand there, totally flummoxed, wondering how your narco, who had just recently professed his undying affection, and how all your mutual friends could suddenly be so cold and overtly hostile to you. What have you ever done to any of them?

You could find one or two of them to say they're really your mates because they're going to ask you all kinds of personal questions, and you're going to answer them because you're so puzzled about what's going on because you want someone—anyone—to help you make sense of it. But for you, they're not there. They dig on behalf of the narco and see a) how well the devaluation is going and b) if there is something the narco wants to do to subvert you or to refute what you may say. Don't forget, and they're there to protect the narco. The narco is their world, just like it was yours, just a short time ago.

He's trying to turn anyone he can against you—friends, family members, even infants. For him, it's not about sanity or doing what's right for the girls, and it's about winning. It's just about killing you. It's about shaming you for being a woman and for wanting everything that you need. He resents you, he's upset at you, he hates you, and it's not because of what you've really done, but because of who you are and who you're not.

He's going to separate you from everyone you meet, or he's going to try. Whether he can drive you over the breaking point, it's just another evidence of how unfit you are. And he's never going to feel guilty for something he does to you, and it's all going to be your fault. He's trying to do the discard in the worst moment ever, or in the most drastic manner possible, and he needs to multiply the cut a thousand times, and that's what he thinks you deserve. Never mind if you stood by him, stood up for him, fulfilled all his desires, or lost everything for him. Now that the love-bombing is over, what he feels when he sees you is how pitiful you are and how deserving of his disdain.

That's when he actually takes out an irrevocable act to cause a discard, intended not just to end the relationship but to kill you. And that generally has to do with the way you think of your replacement. He might also scheme for you to trap them in the act if he knows he's going to have the most pain for you. But whatever he does, he's going to blame you for it. It's all going to be your fault, and thank god he had the presence of mind to triangulate in a new source.

This new woman—probably a close acquaintance of yours, or maybe a relative of yours—is so different from the other woman in her life. She's great, she's special, and no matter what stuff she does to you or your baby, she's the pinnacle of excellence. She's smarter than you are, she's better than you are, she's more in tune with him than you are, she's certainly up on the ladder of evolution than you are. And if you dare to utter her name with anything but respect and respect, he will come down upon you with all the wrath at his disposal. He wants you, in an odd way, to be pleased with his current source. If you dare to express any feeling, such as rage or confusion, he will double his devaluation towards you before he makes your life a living hell.

But before you find out about the new source, he's going to keep stringing you along, convincing you that if you just changed x, y, and z about your actions, the golden days of your relationship will come back. Why? Why? Since he loves watching you leap through hoops, and most importantly, your hoop-jumping keeps you out of his hair, so that he can go on with his plans. If you call him for some of his narco-behavior, particularly during the devaluation or discard periods, he will use the silent treatment or even take a few steps forward to go with the missed treatment.

It's a way to let him see how little you mean to him. He's trying to treat other people magnanimously in front of you—even people he usually can't stand—to hammer the point home on how even his rivals are worth more than you. You matter less than zero to him, and that's all your fault. Narcissists are beautiful, attractive people who make you feel like you've won some kind of love lottery. But dating a narcissist is a soul-sucking nightmare that's all about loneliness, breaking down your self-esteem, undermining your confidence, punishing you over and over for no apparent reason while trying to dangle a carrot of hope in front of you.

Why we Fall for a Narcissist

At one time or another, all of us will find ourselves dwelling on or healing from a romantic run-in with a narcissist. Suppose it was a brief or long-term engagement. In that case, it's possible that during the relationship post-mortem, you'll ask yourself how you managed to get pulled in by his or her charms, how you ignored all the warning signals, what made you so prone to the enchantments of a cold-hearted manipulator (and sometimes a cheat). It's generally not much consolation to know that these are actually the same questions that Echo's hapless nymph questioned herself after her meeting with the original Narcissus of Greek myth.

Why is it so easy to be Seduced by a Narcissist?

The short answer: nothing the narcissist does or does appears to be, and he or she is very, very good at manipulation—and, at least at the beginning of stuff, very charming and entertaining. The longer response is focused on the analysis of how narcissists work in partnerships. Five lessons science has learned from narcissists. The results are both revealing and cautious. Find the following:

The Same Attributes that Make Someone a Narcissist Account for his Initial Appeal

It's at this point where you should hopefully note that old lesson: don't judge a book by its cover. Narcissists exude self-confidence—a grandiosity fuelled by a heartfelt sense of entitlement—and they will do all they can to make you snow so that you become the admirer they crave. Researcher Mitja Back and collaborators have published experiments to find out why a narcissist makes such a perfect first impression. One of the factors is self-representation. Since narcissists are more about self-validating, they concentrate on appearance, including their clothing, grooming, and accessories. (My own narcissist drove a Porsche and wore very costly clothes.) Few of them are born physically beautiful, but they all struggle to retain a flawless and attractive appearance. Self-presentation also attracts favorable attention to them—whether in a dramatic or dominant style, wawing you with laughter, or captivating you with a shimmering chat, an easy smile, and beautiful manners—because a narcissist wants an audience to succeed.

And that's precisely what the studies revealed. In one sample of 72 freshmen—all meeting for the first time and therefore unfamiliar to each other—the researchers made each of them stand up and present themselves to the community after conducting the Narcissistic Personality Inventory. The others measured each individual in terms of looks, stylishness, attitude, and popularity. The latter was measured by questioning whether the person was likable and whether the observer wished to get to know the person.

Will it surprise you to hear that the narcissists were found the most beautiful and charming? All of us would feel ourselves squirming and nervous when we reveal ourselves to a room full of people, but not the narcissist, who, as the researchers called it, is "socially bold." A second experiment gave another audience a video of self-presentation from the first study, and again the narcissist scored a great deal of notoriety.

Boldness and the Feeling of Superiority Make the Narcissist Seem Attractive and Pretend to be a Good Friend

That's what Michael Dufner and others have discovered in a series of studies. In reality, they sent male participants into the streets of a German city with the challenge of contacting 25 women—random strangers—and getting their phone numbers, email addresses, and other contact details. Study assistants accompanied the men and then interviewed the people they had met, asking if they enjoyed the interaction and the conversation, if they liked the man, and if they were drawn to him. True enough, the more arrogant the guy was the more contacts he made, and the more desirable he appeared to women.

The narcissist clearly knows how to make things happen. Alas, while the show seems to be aimed at the person he or she is with, it's not just about them. It's just about self-affirmation. But it takes longer for the narcissist's wife to find it out.

The Narcissist is a Game-Playing Specialist

Studies suggest that narcissists like partners but choose short-term relationships without commitment. They appear to look for the next bond that matches their desires when they're already in a relationship, so it's quite likely that they're cheating on their current love interest. One of the reasons why narcissists will cause their wives a lot of emotional harm is all the mixed signals: the narcissist needs to be in a relationship—but just on his own terms.

Their type of partnership, including the work of W. Keith Campbell and others, has proven that it is the game-play that gives them the leverage of the partnership and their mate. They enjoy control and defend their autonomy—avoiding true affection and commitment—but they do want your attention and sexual gratification. It's like living in a mirror house, except that the only mirror that matters is the one the narcissist keeps in his palm.

At the conclusion of their article, Campbell and his collaborators were asked whether anybody would be dating a narcissist. They must observe that with the beauty and charisma of the narcissist, it needs the patience to be wise in his or her strategies. They also venture that narcissists can target people who are low in self-esteem—on the surface, narcissists look like major captures, after all—and who are vulnerable to self-doubt. Alas, it's a plain fact that when a genuine person gets mixed up with someone who plays sports, it's a sincere person that's going to get hurt.

At a Technical Level, the Narcissist can be really Nice in Bed

James K. McNulty and Laura Widman's work primarily looks at how narcissism works in the sexual domain—because, as they write, "Having a high-quality sexual relationship is an integral part of having a high-quality romantic relationship." What's fascinating is that, sexually, narcissists are a rather mixed bag. They lack sympathy for their partners, but evidence suggests that empathy is part of a healthy sexual experience. Open contact is part of healthy sex, but the self-focused narcissist is not involved in open communication. They also note that narcissists appear to be sexually abusive and prefer infidelity—a behavior that is adverse to a healthy romantic relationship.

But here comes the seductive force of the narcissist, together with the mental uncertainty he or she will shower about your life: narcissists enjoy women, and they're really concentrated on how successful they are about anything. So being "good in bed" matters a lot to them. In the sexual realm, the narcissistic characteristics that are triggered are an entitlement, exploitation, and an increased sense of skill. McNulty and Widman's marriage happiness research have reinforced all of these conclusions regarding narcissists—both negatives about contact and affection and positive results about sexual abilities.

However, a second analysis by these authors indicated that it was sexual narcissism, not generalized narcissism, that projected infidelity. It is estimated that 25 percent of married men and 20 percent of married women cheat—so clearly, not all cheaters are narcissists. McNulty and Widman found that a sense of sexual superiority, confidence in sexual capacity, and lack of sexual sympathy towards a partner were related to infidelity.

The Narcissist does not Apologize or Forget

There is another reason why the relationship with the narcissist is going to be rocky: according to the work of Julie Juola Exline and others, dispute resolution is almost difficult with the narcissists since they are cynical about the importance of forgiveness on the one side and easily insulted on the other. They prefer to do a cost-benefit analysis where there has been a transgression of some kind in a relationship and usually do not see the benefit of either forgiving or ignoring. They're quick to hang on to a grudge.

How a Narcissist Target and Control You

Narcissists have become self-absorbed. They also control interactions, exploit their loved ones, and engage in manipulative profit-making behavior. We strive to get rid of these fake people, but we still fall prey to their abuse. So how are they going to do this? How do narcissists dominate you? What kind of techniques do they use? Here are five strategies used by narcissists to monitor their targets:

1. They're Hitting Codependents

Narcissists also have success in manipulating people when they are exploiting codependents. "Overall, narcissists seek out those with characteristics of codependence," states Tom Gagliano, Relationship Specialist. "The narcissist emphasizes the vulnerabilities of the codependent, that they are conditioned to feel that it is their fault or that they are responsible for correcting any dissatisfaction throughout the partnership. The companion is terrified of the narcissist to the point that they lose their sense of themselves by trusting in all the distortions of the narcissist."

2. They Make you Feel Unique about it

These self-centered people often go out of their way to make others feel special—not because they actually admire something about the person, but because they exploit it. "In their relationships, narcissists often gain control of others by playing with a person's (very understandable) desire to feel special and highly valued," says Clinical Psychologist Forrest Talley. "The narcissist might say, for example, 'Though I just met you, it is obvious to me that you are incredibly bright and competent. I have a very small group of people, much like you, who I want to stay in touch with... I want you to be part of that group. Only give me your phone number, and I'll add it to my special black book.' (Sound ridiculous? That's it because that's what a narcissist told me years ago... no, not a patient)."

3. They're Using Shock, Anxiety, and Guilt

Narcissists continue to take control over people in their lives by evoking difficult feelings. "After a period of 'grooming' someone for a close relationship, the narcissist moves on to use shock, fear, and guilt to maintain control," Talley explains. "The outrage and awe come from the over-the-top, emotionally fraught tantrums that erupt when a mate (spouse or lover) does something that disappoints the narcissist. Most rational people find such dramatic responses stressful and unusual, so they begin to work hard to prevent a repeat show."

4. They're Gaslight

Narcissists are often commonly gas lighters, which means they are expert manipulators. "Gaslighting is the tactics of narcissists, sociopaths, and psychologists," says Christine Scott-Hudson, Certified Psychotherapist. It is a narcissistic activity built for self-giving and also for sport. It's built to weaken, deceive, and destabilize the victim. Gaslighters can argue that they said anything or did something you know they said or did. They're going around the universe unhappily."

5. They're Playing Hot and Cold Football

In the end, selfish people are also apt to play sports. "One of the ways narcissists try to control you is by playing manipulative hot and cold games," says Adina Mahalli, Master Social Worker. "One week, they're going to flatter you to get you to do what they want; the next week, they're going to use violence. The bad moments are interspersed with positive moments so that you do not even know that you are being fooled. The only way to defeat this is to be vigilant when it comes to flattery and positivity. They take a move with a grain of salt and don't let love-bombing be a kind of extortion to you. Niceties aren't meant to be conditional."

Be conscious of these five common techniques of narcissists. If you suspect you've been killed or threatened by these manipulators, do what you can to get them out of their reach. This could mean breaking ties with friends or family members—but that's all right because your mental wellbeing and well-being are on the line, and that's always a priority.

Don't be an Easy Victim for a Narcissist

If you've found yourself a survivor of narcissistic violence, here's the truth: none of it was your fault, and narcissists are the greatest emotional abusers. Chances are you've heard about Narcissistic Personality Disorder so far, but someone doesn't have to have a full-blown NPD case to have the narcissistic characteristics to make them risky to get interested.

It could almost appear like you weren't involved with him, rather that he was involved with you. One day you flirted with this man who you thought was amazing, and the next thing you knew, you were in an immediately serious and dedicated relationship, and you can't remember exactly how that happened.

This is because narcissists are the masters of survival. It's because they have the sixth sense to recognize people with personality characteristics that make them more likely to fall to the charismatic person of the narcissist and to hang around to take care of them long though they show their repulsive inner self. This is where learning how to deal with a narcissist will motivate you to get them out of your life.

But do you know the symptoms of narcissistic personality disorder? If you can associate with the attributes of the 7 points below, you might be at a greater than normal risk of being pursued by a narcissist.

1. You Have Something the Narcissist Wants (Money, Power, Position, Lifestyle)

There is a special dynamic that comes into play in a partnership where a narcissist is engaged. It begins with a hook—a fantasy, sometimes one you believe is for you, but it's just about power for the narcissist.

Often the narcissist will come off as supportive, and then when things don't work out, the table will turn on you. If you've caught up or managed to get him to take action, the stress just escalates.

2. You have a Caregiver's Nature and a Strong Need to Help Others

The partnership appears to be a match made in heaven for a moment, but it's a short ticket to hell. The generosity and goodness of the caretaker are reflected in the early stages of the relationship. The giver has others to do so because being the core of the world fits perfectly for the selfish desires of an emotional vampire. Yet as the relationship grows more personal, the narcissist consumes the time, attention, and money of the relationship while maintaining power.

3. You have a Compassionate, Empathetic Disposition

Narcissists have a justification behind all that happens in their lives, and it is really their own fault. Of course, you listen, and you want to help, but if you hear yourself thinking, "I was just trying to be nice..." more and more frequently, and if any of you get used to it, odds are there's a bad dynamic at hand. In reality, empathic personalities and caretaker forms are ideal candidates for emotional vampires.

4. You Grew up in a Dysfunctional Environment

Your past can make it hard to spot border violations when they happen, which may lead you to disregard your gut instincts whenever anyone breaks your trust. Narcissists don't like borders. Suppose a person has an inability to set them, hold them, or take responsibility after one has been abused. In that case, the predatory form detects the vulnerability and uses it to their benefit. Often narcissists commit valiant deeds; however, instead of promoting their partner's individuality or empowerment, they utilize their support as a method of establishing dependency.

5. You are Lonely and Feel a Desperate Need to Find Love

Find a desire, satisfy a need" is the slogan of the narcissist. An individual with poor self-esteem is simpler to manage than anyone with a strong sense of self-confidence. At first, the force sounds nice, so it may be mistaken with love, yet the narcissist is incapable of honesty. Slowly the passion wanes, and the cold, calculating demeanor leaves you asking what went wrong and seeking to find the caring person you thought you met.

6. You Willingly Accept Blame — even for Things You didn't Do

If the relationship deteriorates, narcissists use shame to "prove" that you are the issue. Empathetic and emotional people are highly vulnerable to gambling as a function of their reflective nature. By redirecting your focus to something you have "wrong," done, the narcissist distracts people away from their own unhealthful conduct.

7. Avoid Conflict and Confrontation

Narcissists prey on paranoia and use it to build smoke screens and mirrors. Non-confrontational individuals are always fearful of abandonment, shame, or something that could contribute to the end of an important friendship. When narcissists respond aggressively, these fears are triggered by those who are bent backward to keep things orderly and peaceful. Counter-intuitively, the more confrontation you stop, the more appealing you become to a narcissist.

You wouldn't have to be a survivor yet. Draw from what you've learned from your past and empower your instincts so that in the future, you'll know how to stop another narcissist if you're targeted. Listen to your intuition, trust your heart, and know that if it's too good to be true, it's a chance.

PART 3: RECOVERING FROM NARCISSIST ABUSE

How do I Heal from Cognitive Dissonance after a Narcissistic Relationship?

Cognitive Dissonance (CD) is the frustration that happens when we don't grasp the acts or conduct of our own or anyone else. We don't understand that anything about these behavior violates our beliefs about ourselves, about them, or about people and the universe. We may minimize discomfort in three ways: change our actions, our values, and/or our memories.

Ns is a specialist in reducing the shipload of CDs that would arise if they could see themselves without protective blinkers. They usually do this by allowing reflexive use of exaggeration, projection, and denial-an an extraordinary and breathtaking capacity to forget details and re-shape memory and truth to meet their needs. And just by lies. Are they really' forgetting, or are they really trying to? It's new. It doesn't matter to you. It's the same thing about you.

For instance, you've just made a novel, out-of-the-box idea to your manager about how to cope with a complicated problem that affects everyone on the team. You have presented a very unique and innovative solution to the issue, but with a very good chance of succeeding. Your manager considers this for a second, and looks to you straight-faced and says, "I think we should do this." She continues to propose the Same plan of action you've just proposed. However, she proposes this-to you, right after you've suggested it! -as fresh ideas and reflections of her own. She also advises that you take the notes! If you say, "You know, do you think we should do what I just suggested? "(As you would have done the first few times), she's going to look at you blankly.

She's acknowledged the importance of your advice, can't handle the CD by knowing that you've come up with a brilliant concept that's going to save the day all. The positive ideas come from her! -and now she just instantly-somehow-makes these thoughts her own. You're gob-smacked the first time this happens and frankly don't know what to do about it, but after a few occasions and bringing stuff together about other odd facets of her actions, you're beginning to understand.

Non-Ns strive to minimize the CD they experience in this kind of situation by different kinds of mental gymnastics-rationalizations, etc. When we exhaust all the other options and confess to ourselves that (incredible as it seems) someone is actually re-writing history as they go (always in a manner that flatters themselves and absolves them of any blame or deficiency), we begin to realize that the person we're working with has some very odd things going on and cannot be trusted.

We begin to understand how they can depend so strongly on us and need us so desperately, still not be able to respect us-not only us or others but ourselves. In reality, the more positive ideas we have and the stronger our job, the more they feel the need to devalue, verbally harass, and undermine us. Colleagues who have found that they begin to make subtle comments out of respect for us are commendable. At that point, we should either avoid being helpful (at this point, they may be nicer to us), affirm their distortions (tell them how smart they are and how much you've gained from them-that is, drink the kool-aid, or make them think we have), endure their disrespect and utter lack of concern for us or end the partnership. We should try to encourage them to understand themselves, too. I tried this incredibly difficult and risky, and I made them hate me more.

Unfortunately, the operation of defense mechanisms is usually not that simple or easy to detect. It could take a long time if this kind of stuff is new to us. We spend all sorts of time wondering why they don't appear to appreciate our job, wondering, challenging ourselves and our assumptions, and even starting to doubt our own comprehension and memory and vision.

This is bad enough in a professional relationship, and once you realize the intense defense processes at work in narcissism, you will miss a lot of sleep. When you're in a romantic relationship with someone, it's a lot tougher. We've got a lot at stake, and our mental gymnastics are getting serious.

We can't help seeking brief comfort by drinking the N kool-aid-sometimes over and over. They are nice and sweet, no matter how unethical their acts are-because they are sometimes, and when it's good, it's so good and comforting to us. We seek comfort in the same friendship that is causing us agony. But then the CD returns, even at 'normal hours, causing considerable emotional and, in many instances, serious physical distress-after we have been seriously injured many times. Things may be going fine, but it's our unconscious prods to remember to keep on watch. Dreams and nightmares tend to say it as it is, that physical discomfort and unease continue to arise in their presence, or even when we think about them. We may have nausea and fear. Listen to your body, man!

We may be going the way of trying to justify it to ourselves-but. This is both complicated and risky. And ultimately, we see that their needs-their essential lies-will still override our interest when their egos or reputations or pride are challenged. Or if they want anything and care for us is in the way, and our options are made clear at that point.

We put up with it, dwindling ourselves poorly and putting ourselves at great risk-because they're going to chuck us under the bus when it suits them. We're going to stay in the situation and drink the kool-aid-either obviously or honestly. Or we're going to get out.

How are we healing? By knowing what's going on with them. And then realizing that they are what they are, that we're not at fault, recognizing that saving them comes at too high a cost, and accepting that in any case, we're over our heads. Over everything by running out of here. And then by not worrying about it, particularly if we have difficulty believing that certain people have little to no guilt or compassion. It's a very tough thing for some people to consider. That was because of me. It's already there.

The Healing Process

Narcissist Personality Disordered men and women are so difficult to connect to since they are incapable of truly knowing you and incapable of caring about you and your emotions. The same is true of their offspring. But I've been bringing together the stuff that has helped me cope with the NPD/ASPD Mask for 47 years. Remember that they are emotionally ill and unable to adjust where they can have a mature, positive, caring, and loving relationship.

Here are some of the items that I find to be useful in knowing and maintaining coping mechanisms following the Narcissist's final discard or quitting them. You're continuing the trip on the road to recovery.

It's not your fault! In this marriage, you did nothing wrong to deserve this mental, verbal, sexual, or physical violence. You can move ahead to marry someone else and enjoy a satisfying relationship, but they will never be able to do so effectively.

You're not alone in this. I know that you feel alone and alone because your support systems have never lived behind closed doors of the NPD then they don't appreciate your spouse's incredibly nuanced and dishonest actions or something else you've had to experience. That's why I'm here to help you get through quitting the NPD and healing.

Educate Yourself on NPD

Discover all the characteristics and deceptive habits of the NPD, so you can avoid them and any potential NPD you encounter from becoming a survivor. This was the most important step to complete for me. You're a kind and compassionate guy; otherwise, he wouldn't have targeted you because he doesn't have those characteristics. To get you into their fold, they "Love-Bombed" you into believing that you had the same beliefs, interests, and dislikes ambitions, and desires. They tell you, in truth, that you are "soulmates! "They tell you that all of you are so close and in love, so why wait, and you'll soon move in or get married. You need to educate yourself about what they're doing, how they're doing that, and why they're doing it. Now there are so many books, posts on the internet, and Quora is a wonderful source of learning their warped attitudes and thought. They're so different from the normal" behavior of a human being.

Self-Assessment

Evaluate If you were able to get sucked in their twisted & tangled web of deception and disinformation! It's not your fault that they are emotionally ill and deemed to be toxic. Yet, it will make you realize how you've been tricked into their culture. I had a wonderful friendship with my dad, so it was hard for me to accept my husband's relentless frustration with me. His love-bombing was because my parents were in love in real life, so it felt like they were on the surface. Yet behind closed doors, there was nothing but False LOVE and pure lies! You must realize why they have scammed you.

If you have children, then write down all incidences for each child that you can recall so that you can hopefully demonstrate how inept they are as a parent. They don't love your kids, nor do they care for their children. So I'd recommend you get full custody of your kid with no custody. Our courts are not up-to-date on these behavioral personality issues. This way, when diagnosing you, you have a witness and proof of how you have been handled, which can give the courts the edge of bending on your side, including all phone numbers, emails, other people who heard things, notes, email, and pictures explaining their actions. He's going to lie to the judge in court and think nothing about it. You've got to be prepared.

Seek out a doctor, preferably a doctor who has improved understanding of NPD behavior. It took me three years of weekly counseling to understand and recover from extreme depression, Complicated PTSD, significant chronic stress-related disorders, and Trauma Bonding (Stockholm Syndrome) induced by 47 years of NPD life.

Find an experienced attorney who knows NPD while you're going through a divorce. Also, strive to get the child's full custody because the NPD is not a responsible mom. They don't care or love the boy. They just want the kid to get back to you so they can make your life miserable. It's hard, but you've got to be entirely non-reactive for their actions. If they're going to get a response out of you, they enjoy it. But don't respond to something they do, even though you're horrified at what they say and do. Often don't confront them about their NPD characteristics; they don't care for you or how you feel. You need to understand that he's got 100 percent of you.

If you plan to leave, you don't need to go to No Contact when you dropped off the face of the earth. This means that under no conditions are you talking to them, calling them, writing them, or delivering any texts to them. Make them speak to your counsel about this. They're trying to do something to try to get you out. Avoid "all contact." means you're going to break off all contacts with them and move on in your life. The NPD is extremely aggressive and is known to be a master at exploiting and getting you back, which is why I suggest No Interaction because it is the most viable way to escape the NPD.

Why is no Contact Advised?

Once they are in touch with you, they will force you to come back, and their penalty will be harder when you come back. Since you left them once before, they're more determined; you won't abandon them a second time! It is also advised that you update all the passwords to your phone and to your computer. Changing the door locks, get new credit cards, a new mobile phone number, don't write, or even speak to them. Don't leave a hint of where you went to launch your new life.

You Deserve Joy and Pleasure

Don't close the door to a new guy in your life who will cherish the way a woman or a man should be loved. However, you need to find the time to get into a new relationship, and you need to recover. If you enter into a new relationship before you recover, you are likely to enter into another relationship with a narcissist. When you go through these steps, and complete your treatment, try to take the time to get back to yourself. It normally takes 18–36 months to recover. Don't panic if it takes longer. You're going to recover a bit older, but a lot smarter. You're going to get the confidence back. Allow them time to recover. Eventually, you need to unlock your soul's door. You're not going to shut it down forever.

What Made Me Safe?

What makes me strong are the two responses that teach me and trust God.

Educate Yourself on NPD

First of all, I've been arming myself with the awareness of NPD symptoms so that I can identify the signs clearly and learn how to run the other way should you see someone like this in the future. I read everything I could about the subject. It made me understand that once they get a full NPD blown, they're unlikely to get better.

Great Faith in Religion

The second quality I have discovered is my strong faith in believing God. God has given me the courage to survive what I've been through. As a result, I am now equipped with a lot of information on the recognition of characteristics related to Covered Narcissistic Personality Antisocial Personality Disorder. I grew up imagining my future as a college professor, but my life has changed drastically, and I'm learning to look at the bright side of my life. God has given me the opportunity to write and share my thoughts with others who are suffering, and I will support them to find their way to healing. If I can help improve my life, that's the 47 years I've wasted!

On Your Recovery Path!

Good luck to you on the way back to the journey of healing. Don't think if the time is shorter or longer. You can develop PTSD Complex, which is a post-traumatic stress disorder. Very definitely, if you are in a long-term relationship with the NPD, you are trauma bonded (Stockholm Syndrome). Don't let that intimidate you. It can be difficult, but it's important to understand and communicate with a trained therapist who understands personality problems, Nuanced PTSD, and Trauma Bonding.

They never loved you or cared about your feelings. They're incapable of ever loving you, and they could care less for your feelings. They're incapable of ever respecting you or even their children. They don't think for any of your emotions if you're lonely, upset, confused, angry, and they lack human sympathy. They're not successful parents, so try to get custody of the children. The only reason they want children to be in the care of you!

CONGRATULATIONS!

The NPD left you in the first step of quitting or becoming blessed. You are no doubt the target of the NPD, but the lone NPD SURVIVOR!! Best of luck to you, and you're strong. You deserve to be cherished and loved again! I'm going to pray for you if you get in touch with me.

9 7 9 8 7 3 2 0 5 0 1 9 6